IN THE FOURTH WORLD

IN THE
FOURTH WORLD

poems by

SANDRA M. GILBERT

with an introduction by Richard Eberhart

The University of Alabama Press
University, Alabama

Library of Congress Cataloging in Publication Data

Gilbert, Sandra M
  In the fourth world.

  I. Title.
PS3557.I34227I5   811'.5'4   78-11144
ISBN 0-8173-8527-4

ACKNOWLEDGMENTS

Grateful acknowledgment is made to the following magazines, in which some of the poems in this book were first published:

Bachy: "A Dream of Pearls."

The Beloit Poetry Journal: "Widow," "Accident," "The Thoreau Pencil," "The Giant Rat of Sumatra."

Calyx, a Journal of Art and Literature by Women: "3 A.M."

Epoch: "Wood," "The Dream of the Red Chamber," "Suicide (2)" (as "Suicide"), "The Milk Dream," parts 1–4 of "Five Meditations on One Who is Dead" (© 1969, 1973, 1975, 1976 by Cornell University).

Epos: "Grandmother," "Black Cow," "Suicide (1)" (as "Suicide"), "The Fireflies" (as "The Dream of the Fireflies").

GiltEdge: "Shell Collecting," "Old Woman."

Hard-Pressed: "Dawn."

Isthmus: "Spring," "In the Fourth World."

The Nation: "Eating Fish," Part 5 of "Five Meditations on One Who Is Dead" (as "The Dream in the Snow"), "After A Death."

NewLetterS (a "Beyond Baroque Foundation Publication"): "The Dream of the Sun," "The Grandmother Dream."

New Moon: "The Dream of Heraclitus," "The Dream of the Death-pill."

The New Yorker: "Her Last Sickness" (© 1969, *The New Yorker* Magazine, Inc.).

Poetry: "The Suits," "The Dream of Shooting Stars," "The Fog Dream," "The Intruder" (as "The Dream of the Intruder").

Poetry Northwest: "The Dream of My Daughter," "Getting Fired, or 'Not Being Retained,' " "The Vengeance Dream."

Poetry Now: "The Cassandra Dream," "The Dream of Lockjaw," "The Dream of the Dog," "The Dream of the Flyway," "Vampire."

Prairie Schooner: "Bad News," "One Shoe" (© 1974 by the University of Nebraska Press).

Seneca Review: "Mafioso," "Doing Laundry," "11 P.M.," "At the Cocktail Hour."

The Smith: "Cook."

Stoney Lonesome: "Blue," "The Dream of the Blue Elevator."

Grateful acknowledgment is also made to Random House, Inc. for permission to quote from W. H. Auden's poem "Consider," in *The Collected Poems of W. H. Auden,* copyright © 1945.

CONTENTS

INTRODUCTION

In the title poem at the end of this book Sandra Gilbert is not satisfied to name only a fourth world but names others up to a seventh, a mystical number. All through her work she is alert to escape, to escapes and discoveries. Her poems are not mystical, but are impulsively, vividly implanted in the real, in present realities. She makes a sheen and fretwork behind which lurk primordial fears. A prime value in her work is to make us feel these fears. She is probably the most outspoken fear-poet of the times. The actual world is threatened repeatedly by dark forces behind appearances.

There is an unseen intruder "delicate and / tremendous as a shard of ice / falling into each eye." In "The Fear of the Night" she is seized by "the fear of the night like an immense bird—/ an owl, a hawk, a predator." In "The Vampire" the vampire is "ancestor / monstrous & inevitable / as a chromosome." There is a giant rat in Sumatra which is "elementary." When a tire blows out ("Accident") "the invisible wolf who lives inside / will come howling out." There are "Five Meditations on One Who is Dead" ending *"Nothing will ever be over."* Note "Bad News," "Traffic Jam," two poems on suicide.

In the last two sections there are more escapes, and more discoveries. At times she becomes surrealistic as in "At the Cocktail Hour." Her work is written in excitement, it gives off positive realizations, sometimes frenetic. There are charming poems like "Tailors" and "The Thoreau Pencil." The section entitled "The Dream Work" has highly fashioned poems of escape and discovery, a remarkable group. Throughout her work she gives a lithe array of verbal skills, intensities, perturbations, inabilities to think there is much redemption, realizations of our plight, some glimpses of hope, mostly large awarenesses of fear and inconclusible reality. She gives us her vision of the human condition, and it is strongly felt, intensely realized in poems the reader finds it hard to escape. They discover themselves in the memory, as well as in their initial impact.

Hanover, N.H.   RICHARD EBERHART

for my mother, Angela Mortola,
and my husband, Elliot Gilbert

GETTING FIRED,

OR

"NOT BEING RETAINED"

I

> . . . nearer that day
> Far other than that distant afternoon
> Amid rustle of frocks and stamping feet
> They gave the prizes to the ruined boys.
> W. H. AUDEN

GETTING FIRED,
OR "NOT BEING RETAINED"

A letter came in the mail from the Vice President of Crucial Events.

Though I tried not to open it, it got out of its envelope
like a secret agent who slips through a door when no one is looking.

The letter regarded me gravely and took stock of me as if it were an
uncle who had not seen me for twenty years.

Then it said: "Due to circumstances"—and something else I didn't
                                                    hear—
decisions have been made" it said "requiring that
and so in accordance with all established procedures you
are not being retained in your present position—that is—"
the letter took a quick puff of a cigarette
and grinned (an engaging grin, like the grin of a movie actor
who makes his fortune from his teeth and hair and lovable
                                                    shoulders)—
"That is—" said the letter— "You're fired!"

"Awfully sorry to have to transmit this bad news"
the letter added, seeing my dismay,
"but that's how things are, you know."

I wasn't bothered. At least, I didn't think I was.
I went into the garden and sat down among
my old friends the rhododendrons and drank some coffee.
The rhododendrons held out five-fingered clusters like
new green stanzas they were writing—"What
do you think of this?"—and
I thought well of them and I was calm.

But in the meantime, while I wasn't looking, the letter
took possession of the house. The letter
stretched out on the livingroom sofa and asked for a newspaper,
which it scrutinized with eyes of steel.

"What's all this shit?" asked the letter sternly
when my children left their sweaters on the kitchen floor
or my husband played the phonograph too loud.

The letter unpacked its suitcases and hung up
an astonishing number of fancy jackets
(all dark tweeds, most
from Brooks Brothers and J. Press)
in my bedroom closet. The letter
sent people on errands and ordered special
delicacies from the supermarket—for its diet was
unusual: it liked the wings of newhatched chickens,
the legs of live crabs, oysters white as
eyes, and carrots whose scream (when they
were ripped from the ground)
was recorded and verified by experts.

The letter took over my study and replaced all the books
with volumes from its own collection, all
black paperbacks, all untitled

At last I couldn't stand
to be in the same house with the letter,
watching it raid the refrigerator,
seeing it read its black books,
and now I spend most of my time beneath the rhododendrons,
thinking careful thoughts—
"If first I—
then perhaps I—
after which, of course,
and so forth—"
while the letter scrapes carrots in the kitchen
for my children.

But the children,
bless them, have got used to the letter,
as though it really were a badtempered old uncle
with whom they have lived all their lives.

EATING FISH

eating fish and admiring the beautiful white bones
like a belt of bleached bobby pins ingeniously
arranged to hold flesh together
by someone who had nothing better to do
during long mornings at sea

eating fish and tasting the sea-colored
juices and wondering who is swimming
in whom right now   am I in the fish
or is the fish in me?   and

eating fish and worrying about dying
like Sherwood Anderson
with a beautiful thin bone
like the tiny cry of a dolphin
splitting my throat

11 P. M.

The smoke from twentyfive cigarettes
hangs in the livingroom like a very complicated noose.
Three moths are pasted to the bathroom wall,
three dead leaves getting suntanned by nothing. . . .

This is the hour when the mirrors long for revolvers
and the bathtub wishes to be filled with blood.
This is the hour when the wife confesses to the husband
and the burglar draws on his rubber gloves,
testing the fingertips for holes.
This is the hour when the lamps grow beards
and the bushes huddle together, ashamed of the darkness.

The dull walls of the house move nearer:
they mutter advice in thick cottony voices.
Headless and armless, they embrace the carpet.
Trembling, they stroke the sofa.

Upstairs, in their weightless beds,
the children are flying away like high clouds.
In the livingroom the words of the parents rise,
the cries of ambulances, keen and close.

3 A. M.

3 A.M. The stench of methane gas in my nostrils—
where does it come from?—
and once again the blank dream
of the intruder with his marble eyeballs.
And a sweetish taste on the tongue—
the taste of death, the gas,
or the delicate kiss
of the intruder?

Down the hall my oldest daughter
trembles in her sleep.
Her feet beat against the sheets.
In her nightmare she's running away again
from the enormous room.
And I too hunch for running: the fear
dazzles, a lightbulb just snapped on,
200 kilowatts of terror.

Have we decided already?
Is it time to go?
Though we thought we were safe in our beds,
though we hardly noticed,
the gas was coiling under the door
and the intruder, stepped from his iron van,
was loading his stacks of black
suitcases into our heads.

THE INTRUDER

At first he's only a breath in the dark,
measuring himself out like a heartbeat,
discreet as the blood that flows and coils in places
we never bother to remember.
                                    At first
he enters through cracks, in the light that leaks
unnoticed under the door from the bare hall
where the bulbs blister the nightlong fears of the children away,
in the damp that shreds the paper from the walls,
in the pane where the window refuses to hold itself together.

At first he's fast, coming and going
like something I thought I saw from the corner of my eye
but it was never there.
                                    At first
he tells himself rapidly as a fairy tale
already told a hundred times.

But then we know he's here. Both of us know.
At once. You wake. You speak.
There's somebody here. A third breath.
We lie motionless in bed—what is there to do—
imagining and discarding the useless weapons,
that crystal lamp, the old mirror, the lightswitch,
the children, the children.

Someone has of course ripped out the phone.
We are all silent, together, in the dark.

The bed trembles. Yet still you do not move.
But I—at last I open my eyes.
                                    And though
I do not see him (I see nothing)
at last his presence falls upon me, delicate and
tremendous as a shard of ice
falling into each eye.

THE FEAR OF THE NIGHT

I'm walking alone at night.
The moon marks my path like a flashlight,
a dull path, a gray light.

A few stars pierce the sky, fine needles.
A jet chalks a fuzzy line
en route to the north.

It's still, calm.
The trees of the windbreak embrace
their shadows in silence.

When all at once the fear of the night
seizes me,
the fear of the night like an immense bird—

an owl, a hawk, a predator—
swoops over the road.
I want to run but I'm heavy and thick:

I crouch like a bald rock at the edge of the meadow,
I become a naked coat, a shell,
I play dead.

Will they find me in the morning, seething with flies?
The great owl sweeps by, hooting.
I shiver in the grass, I kiss cold stones.

Between cracks in the ground I see
the deep earth cellar where
fierce roots move.

Above me the moon paces coolly,
like a knowledgeable person,
her vagueness the light of pure reason.

VAMPIRE

"Good evening, I am Count Dracula"

I fly in out of the night
with a swish of lace curtains
two clouds parting
black sun between
because I want to own you

my fangs sink in like needles
I inhabit your veins
when you wake sighing at white
sunrise
you won't remember
the long night
the singing

I will always have been there
your perfect dead batwinged
ancestor
monstrous & inevitable
as a chromosome

THE GIANT RAT OF SUMATRA

"Matilda Briggs was not the name of a young woman, Watson,"
said Holmes in a reminiscent voice. "It was a ship which is associated
with the Giant Rat of Sumatra, a story for which the world is not yet prepared."

Poor Watson, you never met him?
Befuddled in foggy London
you wandered the labyrinthine streets.
Down by the docks you found a violin

floating in murky waters,
waters blue-black and bruised by
too many nights. Later,
in your stuffy room,

you prescribed cocaine—
cocaine for the brain!—
but your prescriptions were intricate and
indecisive, like bad philosophy.

Days passed, days and days.
You were always lonely.
Medical metaphysician,
you could never figure anything out.

But Watson, dear Watson,
all the time, there he was!
There he still is!
The leaves part,

they're purple, they rustle.
The jungle moans with excitement.
The natives are restless tonight.
They have drums fiercer than violins,

their heads glisten like horsehair sofas,
heads on stakes.
Another hour and he'll come out.
Already the ceremonial fires are lit.

12

And Watson, he's so much bigger
than the ship Matilda Briggs.
His great fangs are taller than masts,
his tail is a sail heaving him along,

he walks like twentyfive earthquakes.
Sumatra bows before him.
Tomorrow he'll swallow the Thames,
he'll gobble Big Ben,

Westminster will cower,
Her Majesty will shudder,
and then—and then—
Ah Watson, don't you know him?

He's gray and massive like the fog.
His eyes gleam like copper kettles.
His ears are dark, so dark,
and his tongue so elementary.

ACCIDENT

Accept the fact, the tire is going to blow:
there on the highway the car will begin to sway;

for a moment things will wobble, an unsteadiness
will take possession: then the veering, then the incoherence,

and the invisible wolf who lives inside
will come howling out.

HER LAST SICKNESS

Sailing the long hot gulf
of her last sickness,
out past the whispering beach,
she saw the town lights dim.
What were those voices shouting in her head?
She was their sentence, they were hers.
Words ripped at her ribs
like multiplied hearts, until
she drowned in that intolerable pulse.

Now riding the slow tide
she's dumb as driftwood, sheds
her last light skins of thought
easily as October.
Mouthing the great salt flow,
black with it, white with its foam,
she's picturesque—no more than a design
on the packed sand, hieroglyph
from another land.

AFTER A DEATH
for my father

I am far away from you.
In my front yard the uncontrollable rain
coats leaves and bark
with a medicinal, protective sheen.

What I inherit is impossible:
a car I can't drive,
empty coats in a closet,
a useless middle initial.

I am astonished by my calm.
Have you really left me no pain?
The enormous sky, floodlit by thunder,
recalls your cold home—

the comforting grass,
the black socket of stone
in which you are fixed
like a blind eye, directionless.

FIVE MEDITATIONS ON ONE WHO IS DEAD

You rise and set.
You sink with Ra.
You rise with Isis,
rise with the morning
ship of the sun.

—from *The Egyptian Book of the Dead*

1

I dreamed that I had Corn Fever.

They told me this rare disease occurs
when you eat too much corn, and choke on it,
and the tough little kernels enter your bloodstream,
and you're corny all over.

I was. I was in great danger.

Yellow and hot, the dangerous corn
spun through my arms until they ached.
In the dark of my stomach corn seethed.
The walls of my heart were corny.

"We must save her before it's too late,"
the doctors cried.

My thousand ears were ripe with listening,
my tassels drooped and wept.
I was a corn field in the sun,
growing and weeping my shattered seeds.

I wasn't thinking of you, O Orpheus.
I believe I was thinking of a young man I once knew,
dead now (he was never very wise),
dead now, and kernels of snow
are falling in his eyes.

2

17

There are these
red branches of my eyes
leaning swaying

and among them
the leaves that are my pupils
look for you:

white of my eyes,
snow in the sockets,
falls upon you,

my tears are seeds
from which you grow
(though you are dead)

(dead
you grow more dead
more dead today than yesterday).

I extend myself over you,
my eyes
rustle as the wind pours by.

Today,
tomorrow,
I shade you with my down-turned glance.

3

In my dream Professor Shrimp
fought the wolf that was you,
struggling and grappling,
Professor Shrimp in his pink tweeds,
you snarling and gray
with the death-fur on you.

Nobody won.

You were dead
before the dream began.

4

Though you are dead
I imagine the glass girl
slides still
down the white slope
of your mind.

Translucent
she skis toward you,
always arriving,
arms outstretched.
Ah my dear,

what words did she say to comfort you
when you first embraced her
and saw the hillside
glittering
through her eyes?

Outside my window the intricate
snow of my childhood blooms again,
first snow, motionless kingdom of

branches black and white, ice and light . . .
And last night in my dream
you too appeared again,

though God knows you have now
been dead two years, two years
beneath the molding snow,

but there you were, again, intolerant
of my life. *You left,*
I said. *You stood in the doorway.*

Tears drifted across my cheeks like snowflakes,
melting, freezing, freezing, melting—
your face or mine? I wasn't sure.

But it wasn't over, you said.
Nothing will ever
be over.

BAD NEWS

The clock eats another hour
like an amateur magician in a rundown hotel
who has no audience
but goes on doing tricks anyway.

In the boardinghouse next door
where the chambermaid has just
finished the third floor bedrooms,
bad news begins to emerge.

Bad news steals out of a bureau drawer
like a black scarf that nobody noticed,
like an irrepressible yawn,
like the white tentacle of a potato
left too long in the cupboard under the sink.

Bad news invades the neighborhood
while the chambermaids
lean helpless on their brooms
and the hotel managers chase it
shouting and spraying something ineffectual
from an aerosol can.

Bad news arrives in the lobby
where the singleminded clock is performing
with skillful fanatical hands,

and the clock swallows it
as if it were a rare brandy.

TRAFFIC JAM

The cars are all limping and
the trucks suffer from a strange
form of palsy.

Something hangs in the air with
ten heads that turn even air
to stone:
it dangles smiling
like a scientist who has not yet
invented death
but is on the verge of a
great breakthrough:

whimpering
we rub the steering wheel
and beg for feathers.

MAFIOSO

Frank Costello eating spaghetti in a cell at San Quentin,
Lucky Luciano mixing up a mess of bullets and
calling for parmesan cheese,
Al Capone baking a sawed-off shotgun into a
huge lasagna—
                    are you my uncles, my
only uncles?

            O Mafiosi,
bad uncles of the barren
cliffs of Sicily—was it only you
that they transported in barrels
like pure olive oil
across the Atlantic?

            Was it only you
who got out at Ellis Island with
black scarves on your heads and cheap cigars
and no English and a dozen children?

No carts were waiting, gallant with paint,
no little donkeys plumed like the dreams of peacocks.
Only the evil eyes of a thousand buildings
stared across at the echoing debarcation center,
making it seem so much smaller than a piazza,

only a half dozen Puritan millionaires stood on the wharf,
in the wind colder than the impossible snows of the Abruzzi,
ready with country clubs and dynamos

to grind the organs out of you.

1/1/76

A rotten night in N.Y.,
the billboards blurred in mist,
the celebrants shivering into subway holes,
steam wreathing the pavements, a parody of dew,

and Times Square, that fat black egg,
time's spheroid, tips in the sleety darkness,
tips, rocks, sways, bulging with bellowing horns—
the house of misrule! the sacred pipes erect!—

till the egg bursts
and the Bicentennial New Year comes with screams:
200 dead Indians, 200 Christs in concrete,
200 slanty-eyed skulls in the Rockies

all rising inscrutable to say—to say—
well, what is there to say?—
and on the California coast gulls spin and squeal,
sentinels over Drake's Bay,

where the great Queen's ship once hung
shining and unself-conscious as a golden egg.

SHELL COLLECTING

At Black Point, collecting shells.
The sky smoke gray,
a few birds tossed in the wind—
dark motes, dark functions
of the eye.

Shells bloom in the tide pools.
Shells scuttle like spirits.
I imagine them clicking and speaking,
a poem of safety,
an epic of multiplicity.

On the cliff the raw grass
winds around itself,
tangling, untangling.
In the gray sea a thousand
storms are drowning.

Beside a cave at water's edge I find
an immense sea anemone,
almost invisible, packed in sand.
It quivers to the touch.
It is so naked I want to kill it.

Stirring still water with a stick,
I see, now, everywhere
anemones without shells
clinging to sand and rock,
silent, enigmatic,

and I long for the certainty of shells.
Can such nakedness be safe?
How should I live
when even the blackest rock
is elastic with life?

VOICES

II

If we had a keen vision and feeling
of all ordinary human life, it would
be like hearing the grass grow and the
squirrel's heart beat, and we should
die of that roar which lies on the
other side of silence.

GEORGE ELIOT

THE SUITS

We're your shadows, your discarded skins,
your dark nurses and your tweedy mistresses.
No matter what you do, we retain you
like the stripped synapses of a computer.

On summer afternoons we exhale you
in the quiet of the closet
while you're practicing the deadman's float
at the country club.

All night
when you lie naked in your bed
(dreaming of feathers)
we bear the imprint of your shape
like the hammock in your mother's back yard.

No matter where you go
we wait for you,
wait and wait, patient
as grandfathers on the porch of a nursing home.

The best of us, the oldest and wisest,
you've almost forgotten:
the sharkskin with padded shoulders that you
put on for your first job interview,
the navy flannel with a special lining
that you wore for your bar mitzvah:

those two
will wait forever,
wait and wait at the back of the closet
where hangers multiply
and it's never morning.

OLD WOMAN

It is as though each day
a thicker curtain falls
between me
and the world's walls,
blurring the sight,
muffling the sound
of things. . . .

Sense clings
to recollection;
the threads of substance
rip apart;
there is no stuff that is not worn and threadbare
in the heart;
no mending of my days or eyes.

Spring comes with piercing cries:
the midnight wail of cats,
the screaming wind,
the birds' demand.
I know there are chick-yellow flowers in the grass,
and that the sky is shining clear as glass,
a pane I cannot pass.

The birds know best:
on worms they feast;
it is their Easter and their passing over.
I mark the calendar—
the week is full of days to celebrate,
dry palms to agitate the light
like pallid banners blown along the street.

Good Friday—Agapé—
the threads are torn and fray,
and Saturday's a dusty shop
whose scornful keeper
knows what I no longer know:
he unrolls Easter
like a bolt of faded calico.

HOMICIDE

The victim oozed astonishment like sweat.
Slowly but irreversibly his fear gathered—
mad mobs shouting in the court of his throat,
the speaking pillar crumbled, in a moment
an age of thought undone, utterly demolished.

His scream, when it came, was of the duck family,
or of the tribe of geese. I was the fierce
reiterated fist of a hill
and a hill and a hill and a hill
that punishes a skyful of those honking beasts.

SUICIDE (1)

Entering
the great cathedral of the bridge,
I watched fat buses labor by,
worms on a winter branch, veer
in the wind at the turnoff, achingly
close to the rail.

          Whose is the shadow
that topples past the wire fence,
and turning fast, in a brisk breeze,
sets out like a sail
across the water?

GRANDMOTHER

Each night I see myself in the white
mirror of sleep—

(is it myself
I see?)

—a face vast and wrinkled as the sea
at evening,

a vague face
withdrawing. . . .

Other faces, small and white and round as
peeled apples

fall from the long dark
face I wear:

my round grandchildren!
One is taking my nose away,

another my lips, a third my cheeks. . . .
In the morning

I find they've moved to California
with all my features intact

and only my eyes are left in
a face that is no longer mine.

COOK

Steam swells and blurs in my kitchen
like skywriting that fades
from sentences to smoke.
————T AT JOE'S

I stir anyway.
All day I portion myself out,
stirring and sifting.
Flour pours in my palms
like a million delicate eyeballs.
I know how to handle it.
I have a recipe for everything
and I beat every egg as if it were
my last chance to make my feelings known.

Beneath my whisk the yolks march
healthy and compliant,
a squadron of yellow petals
blossoming for me alone,
and the whites rise like spirits
standing up and saluting.

Only, on dark afternoons,
when I nap on my cot behind the stove,
I have bad dreams.

Then I meet the beets dressed as warriors,
then the eggs flutter and grow feathers,
and the flour whispers strange equations
as it churns in the bin.
Then the lambchops tear off their paper frills
and curse me,

and the tall green alien legs of asparagus
stalk from the simmering pot
to hunt me down. . . .

SUICIDE (2)

It is June. Night.
The grass vanishes.

Alone on a plateau of shadows
the white roses remain—

creamy, indefatigable,
starring the darkness . . .

O visible wax
works of the clock,

shapes of the scent
of oblivion,

little white moon-mouths
gaping in the darkness,

piranha of the garden—
let me be small, let me be trivial,

let the soil
digest me.

WIDOW

Another night unfurls its million leaves of shadow.

Cars go by on the highway, one and another:
faint hiss of the lights against my skin—
white lights, colder than steel.

I lie so still I am only another leaf.
I lie alone in my bed. I feel no grief.

My bed, still charged with summer,
is hot like a body, hot like sunstruck earth,
hot and flowering around me
with darkness.

ONE SHOE

My twin is gone and I'm useless now,
an unemployed porter in a world without suitcases.

Dead air thrusts a heavy ankle between my flaps.
My laces stir at the wind's cold feet.

Sweat of leather, scuff of life,
if only I could rise and carry myself
away from my shape!

BLACK COW

Almost winter. Still in the field.

I'm bare and heavy as a rock.
I eat the aching stubble, eat and eat.
The rain eats me.

My eyes are bald like the sky
staring at stones.

All day my milk prepares itself:
a flock of white birds
from the south.

THE DREAM WORK

All art is dream, and what the day is
done with is dreaming-ripe, and what art has
moulded religion accepts, and in the end
all is in the wine-cup, all is in the drunken
fantasy, and the grapes begin to stammer.
                                        W. B. YEATS

THE CASSANDRA DREAM

I open my bureau drawer
and there I find
my beautiful cousin Cassandra.
She has a face like old linen,
yellow and soft,
dark hair that streams into the corners,
blank eyes like the eyes of a doll.
I realize she's waited for years in this drawer,
ever since my grandmother put her there.

I beg her to speak,
to tell me all she knows.
I invoke the tie of blood.
But it's no good:
she's motionless, mute, folded away like a sheet.
Only her cold hair, cold as a night river,
grows while I watch,
spills from the drawer,
swirls, tumbles,

drowns me in a dark prediction.

THE DREAM OF THE BLUE ELEVATOR

The blue elevator goes down into the sea
past blue ears of mussels, listening in silence,
past muscular starfish, skinned, scarlet,
hanging on like panicky hands.

Down, down.
Level one:
this is the level of foam,
where I'm trivial, I utter platitudes.

Words curl from my lips like draggled seaweed.
We're going a lot further, says the operator.
He wears a deep-blue suit, shiny and dark
as though the cloth sweated.

But for him this is just a job
(and not a pleasant one).
Down and down.
Below rock, below sand.

Waves crouch overhead like houses, a watery city.
Level two, level three.
Here sense forsakes me,
here I'm eaten by wishes.

here. . . .
At an indeterminate point
between levels six and seven
I can tell the elevator's broken.

Like something not itself,
like something else (but what?)
it plunges downward,
digging a hole in the ocean.

The operator smiles.
All in a day's work.
He's the bad dream I've always had.
He smiles. *It's just a job.*

Smiles. He feels no shame.
And the odor of my fear
fills the darkening chamber
like some ecstatic cheap perfume.

THE DREAM OF THE SUN

Asleep on the beach, I step onto
the porch of the sun
where my father (seven years dead) sits in
a chair of scarlet wicker.
He smokes a cigar and looks at me calmly.

"I've been reading Nietzsche, Tom Paine, Gautama Buddha,"
he says. "I think I've found the answer."
"Daddy," I cry. "It's been so long!"
He motions to a yellow porch swing.
"Let's talk things over quietly, darling."

"I'm afraid." I tremble at the edge of the porch.
I cling to the railing. Below
black spaces swirl like the sea,
all round us an echoey roar as though
we had entered a giant shell.

"Daddy, I want to go back."
Sand flies tear at my flesh. I'm almost awake.
He throws away his cigar.
He rises sobbing. (He doesn't look well.)
"Sandra, Sandra, don't leave me here!"

THE DREAM OF THE DOG

Who strays all night in the meadow
(he may be a werewolf).
Who has eyes like saucers and iron claws.
Who disappears into the bushes
every time I try to look
(as my shadow disappears when
I try to overtake it).

At midnight I wait in the bare Presbyterian church.
The elders have vanished. The empty pews
shoulder the darkness like patient widows.
I'm alone with the dead—
with the ghosts of the hired man and the weary aunt
whose frail interminable knitting
has been laid aside.

I'm cold, uncertain.
Shall I pray? If I truly pray
will the Dog appear, come from the windy meadow
like a branch blown through a window?
Will I hear the elegant click of his claws
in the center aisle,
the breezy snuffle, the almost inaudible growl?

If I pray
will he turn the bland white light
of his mythy eyes upon me?

THE MILK DREAM

My breasts are full of milk.
They tower above me like peaked rocks
(though no one sucks).
Warily I touch the left nipple.
It's red as a strawberry, feels like rubber,
but rises from a white and stony
promontory.
This is the Not-Me
I think (calm, philosophical).
This hard white wall conceals some valley
tough with its own life.

Yet I long to enter,
to walk into the center of these mountains,
to find the little secret spring where warm milk wells,
not me, but mine.

I rise, I start on the journey.
I'm wearing boots, carrying a knapsack,
climbing, climbing.
The air is cold near the peaks.
There are few houses.
Already the sun has set
and blue winds flow by like tides.
Everywhere doors are closed,
windows made fast for the night.
All closed, all locked against me.

Lonely, I camp among the rocks
at the edge of my body.

THE DREAM OF PEARLS

Oyster-like, fixed upright
in the cold rills and ripples

of my bed, mother-of-pearl,
I meditate on pearls:

snake-thick strings of pearls.
Seed pearls. Fake pearls. Baroque

pearls. Lucent toes
of a saint? Faint

eggs of oblivion? Fish
fruit? Tumors of ice?

Bubbles of extragalactic breath?
Teeth of the moon? I shiver

with the joke of them.
I roll, I bathe in them! I secrete them.

The night wears on.
The stars tread out their distances like wine.

The gulp and spit of the sea
annihilates me.

O pearls—O multiplied fanciful
eyes of the assassin,

I am not amused,
not amused.

THE DREAM OF THE RED CHAMBER

My heart beats heavily.
It is the chamber in which I live:
thick red-brown walls, walls the color of liver
and a system of pumps and valves
I'm too simple to understand.

I sit on an oriental rug in the middle of my heart.
The rug has beautiful markings, red and brown,
like the shell of a rare turtle.
I sit cross-legged and meditate, while
the walls of my heart say *doom-om, doom-om.*

But the beating of my heart distracts me.
Will this motion never stop? This dull symmetry
(first *doom*, then *om),* this bloody earthquaking?
I dream of calm: the cold gray plush of the brain,
the dry white crevices of the spine. . . .

Days pass as I sit in my heart,
bored and alone, wondering how to get out.
After a week I receive a visit from an architect
who promises to redesign the place so I won't mind it:
from a suitcase he produces blueprints, hammers, nails.

My heart stiffens, it freezes into silence.
The red chamber becomes a room in a museum.
Someone pastes a label on the door:
"Red Chamber of the Civil War Period.
Certain Visitors Claim It Is Haunted."

Meanwhile I've gone to live in my skeleton,
a more commodious apartment.

THE DREAM OF HERACLITUS

On the subway I meet Heraclitus.
All is in flux. We're thundering
into Grand Central Station.
"You can never step twice
onto the same train," he says wisely.

His oiled beard twitches with irony,
his toga's dusty as if he just stole it
from some poor widow's linen closet.
"You!" I exclaim.
(Why don't the other passengers see him?)

"Grand Central, Grand Central,
Change here for Times Square,"
cries the conductor.
The train is flowing with people,
people rush in and out like demons.

·Approaching time's square!
I too want to rise,
I want to get off the train,
but I'm gluey with sweat:
I stick like gum to the seat.

Up and down the car
doors open and close, terrible mouths.
I imagine myself transfixed
between black rubber lips,
eaten by the panting *D* train.

I don't move.
With a steely groan, the train moves on.
No Times Square. No more Grand Central station.
"You see what I mean?"
says Heraclitus.

THE DREAM OF MY DAUGHTER

Officious, I begin
to brush my daughter's hair,
which is delicate and fair
as a green young fern.

She cries, she cries out
"Mommy, watch it,
I'm sensitive"—
but I'm unmoved, I'm passionate.

Like a large beaked bird
I tear, I tear,
I claw at her hair,
her hair green-golden,

her hair straw-light,
her hair of Rapunzel,
shredding, feathery,
descending around me,

her hair of pollen
which dissolves as I watch
to a thousand cells,
her hair of bees—buzzing, alive—

her hair of poison,
her hair of sun in the hive,
her hair that is melting like wax:
"Mommy, mommy," my daughter weeps,

but ruthless I rip it away—
"Rapunzel, Rapunzel, let down your hair"—
till the curls stream hollow and clear
like an empty river,

and only a few blonde burrs, a dying bush,
are left in the brush.

THE DREAM OF LOCKJAW

My jaw has become a stone,
my throat is full of needles.
I sink deeper and deeper into the bland
voluptuous sofa, which
enfolds me lovingly as quicksand.
My body arches like an ancient bridge.
Soon I will pass across it from this into that,
bleeding and screaming, a triumphant army.
The ghosts of dead electrons dance on
the horrified white television screen.
I'm self-consciously melodramatic:
strangling, I cry "This is It!"

In the next room the children are working like devils,
absorbed, intense, with tiny chisels.
But by the time they break the delicate silver locks
it will be too late.

THE VENGEANCE DREAM
for Bob Griffin

"Vengeance is mine" saith the Lord.
He rises like steam from my coffee cup,
He rises in my throat like silver blood,
ruthless and metallic.

I'm driving through Thousand Flowers Georgia
with my friend's mother;
she's wearing broken granny glasses,
I'm carrying a dozen maps I can't read.

"Naturally their purses were snatched
(and vice versa)" says my friend's mother.
And the Lord has stolen our blood,
He has changed it to mercury:

a sluggish river, a slow river of retribution,
our blood flows down the hot main street
of Thousand Flowers Georgia
past the wilting flowers;

month by moon it flows away as
the hands of the clock turn and
the maps dissolve in my hands
and the Lord says

"I have taken your revenge,
it will never be yours."
"Where is it?
Won't we ever find it?"

shrieks my friend's mother as she weeps in my arms,
her face in tatters,
her face a sodden
rag of a torn-up granny gown.

THE DREAM OF THE DEATHPILL

I take the deathpill between my lips
like the Eucharist.
It's dry and thin, a cracker that cracks bone,
white like the white of an eye turned up to heaven.

As the thin voluptuous deathpill
dissolves my lips
I hear alarmclocks jangle for the elevation of the Host,
and Uncle Death takes my hand.

He wears a high white chef's cap that blooms at the top
like a cottony cloud on a summer's day.
"This is the best I can do," he says apologetically,
"This is my own recipe."

"It comes to you straight from the ovens
of Black and Black and Black and Black
and Black." His voice trails away,
indecisive and flavorless as a bad cracker.

I murmur polite appreciation
(we're both embarrassed).
He, after all, is the host,
and I the guest.

THE GRANDMOTHER DREAM

My Sicilian grandmother, whom I've never met,
my Sicilian grandmother, the midwife, who died
forty years ago, appears in my bedroom.
She's sitting on the edge of my bed,
at her feet a shabby black bag,
and she speaks a tangled river of Italian:
her Sicilian words flow out like dark fish, slippery and cold,
her words stare at me with blank eyes.

I see that she's young, younger than I am.
I see her black hair gleam like tar as
she draws from her small black midwife's bag
her midwife tools: heavy silver instruments
polished like doorknobs, polished—misshapen, peculiar—
like the knobs of an invisible door.

THE DREAM OF SHOOTING STARS

My house is round & journeys through the darkness like a ship,
unwieldy, thick, tossing the night
from side to side.

Asleep, I peer through the portholes.
There on the water
flash the shooting stars,

darting like moths, like nervous insects,
like rocks flung by children
in a swift river.

I know they're the souls of
my father, my grandfather, my uncles,
my dead lover,

flashing away,
flashing back,
flashing.

They smile with impersonal white faces,
their eyes abstractions,
their chins silver.

Cold sparks, they shoot by silently,
whispering nothing,
discreet as optical illusions.

I call them in a fading voice—
goodbye, goodbye—
call like a penitent,

call for pardon,
as my round ship
lumbers heavily on.

THE FOG DREAM

Out of the fog
the voice of the clairvoyant speaks
with the precision of a bird:
  You have a few years left.
  You will end in hope.

The listener in the fog is startled.
  I never asked a question.
  Why this answer?
Her words hang in the air, unanswered.
then drift away, slow feathers.

THE DREAM OF THE FLYWAY

I find myself in the Pacific flyway
high high up (no vertigo)
guiding myself by subtle patterns
in the nighttime sky.
One of my legs is banded with iron,
to the other is strapped a message I must deliver.

I'm tense with motion, my body
yearns toward the south.
Above me are clouds like feathers, stars like eyes,
blackness polished on blackness.

For a moment I waver, my wings dip north.
Meteors flash by like bullets.
What's the peculiar message I carry?
"Shoot this bird on sight, dissect the body?"

But as I fly the sky speaks softly,
speaks as my grandmother spoke in the attic room:
"Here there's nothing to fear.
These shapes aren't spooks, they're just your toys."
I'm swift with joy (I'm sure this isn't a dream).
Expert, I fly on, fly on.

The Great Circle is my home.

IN THE FOURTH WORLD

IV

. . . the dark canals are whistling,
whistling, for who will cross to the
other side. . . .

W. C. WILLIAMS

DOING LAUNDRY

I am doing laundry in my laundry room
the washing machine grinds and pumps like my father's heart
it is sick   it is well
sick again   well again

behind the round window your shirts
leap and praise God slowly like gentle souls
and my old brassieres bound like the clean breasts
of antelopes

I am doing laundry in Africa
and overhead the parrots shriek
they encourage me to beat harder
beat the dirt out of the flowers

I am doing laundry in Indiana
my husband the insurance salesman comes in
wanting to know if I would like to buy his new
insurance against laundry

I am doing laundry in the river Styx
I pound and I pound
the shirts disappear
the brassieres dissolve to nothingness

I am a heart doing laundry
and I beat and I pound
until I no longer remember
the color of dirt

SPRING

why do my toes burn
why do my toenails feel
as though they want to fly away
why are the pupils of my eyes dilating and
fluttering like gills

I pass through a long antechamber
where flowers huddle in bunches
whispering secret formulas

my skin is flaking off in patches
leaving green wounds!

blood washes my ears
air pours through my fingers
I'm smaller than an oyster
somebody's going to eat me whole

I see that the appletree in the garden
is wearing a necklace of feathers and
I enter the warm house
like a cell
entering a royal lung

why did I spend the whole winter
hibernating in doorways?

AT THE COCKTAIL HOUR

The nuts shiver in the bowl and crack themselves open—
almonds, cashews, walnuts, peanuts, all
weary of silence, integrity, loneliness.
Within each nut are rooms of yellow and black;
tiny passages where the hands of trees tremble;
alleys of scuttling mice; pinholes, peepholes, mirrors;
flowers trapped among roots; shoes; fingers.
All this has now been freed and floats in the air toward the ceiling
while the nuts lie shining and broken.
Salt pours from their flanks like a bad memory.
The professor of botany frowns, and the host, stirring martinis,
attempts to frame apologies.
Great trees rise from the carpet; leaves whisper; birds
nest in the hair of the visitors.
The hostess is confused, distressed:
what was promised has been revealed at last.

WOOD

Tree flesh,
you move invisibly,
accumulating
toward the sky. . . .

Sneak—
sneaking life,
stealthy and stiff
but furious with sap

deep inside:
cell on cell,
pile on pile
of tree-self

lives and moves
like the movement of a clock,
imperceptible
but real as rock:

oak, walnut, birch,
mahogany—
dead selves, dead cells—
even through all that fixed

ignominy
of chairs and tables,
sun shines,
sun trapped in the grain,

sun whorled and whirled
that speaks the time
when leaves and blossoms
sprang from you like time.

TAILORS
for Elliot

my grandfather the tailor sat in his little dark shop
sewing me together
(twice a day my Sicilian grandmother brought him
platefuls of praise like bowls of spaghetti)

my other grandmother the seamstress basted and hemmed
(her needle traced strange Russian characters
on the rough cloth)

your grandfather the tailor lengthened you
imperceptibly
(he lovingly made you a beard and a *tallis*)

and in the sultry sweatshops of the lower East Side
(where summer swelled like a giant cabbage)
hundreds and hundreds of great aunts
hunched over glittering machines
in the heavy weather
crooning and clucking and
weeping and gossiping

and stitching together the sidewalks
that would stitch us together

THE THOREAU PENCIL

"Thoreau's father was a pencil manufacturer, and young David Henry improved the Thoreau pencil in several important ways."—Arnold Biella

I am not writing with it
right now   you can't buy one
for ready money
anymore   but
I dream   dream of it
(who has not)
the steely graphite
at the center
rock-dark
black-night-lake-surface-dark
inscribing   scribing
the wood around the outside
a fir-tree   a birch-tree
—I don't know the details—
pared down to size

what characters it must write
what clean Romantic
hieroglyphs
pebbles from the shore of Walden pond
(beyond the trailer park)
nut shells   mosquitos wings
tangled branches intricate
and indiscreet
"to glorify God and enjoy him forever"

they say Thoreau could pick up twelve
Thoreau pencils at a time
without looking
like picking up a year   all at once
in a minute

BLUE

Blue has a beard, a tall hat, a watch-chain;
buzzes in the dark, begging to be let out;
clings like grease to the underside of the white table
in the yellow kitchen.
Aquiline as Plato, Blue resolves
to live ascetically forever
on the cliffs of light.

Blue pores over the dictionary,
learning the secret names
of things
and drives a dark car
up the hill toward the cathedral;
wields a purple revolver;
sips red potions for relaxation.

Meeting Blue disguised as an animal
in the quiet yard where summer
builds its earthworks,
I am afraid,
though I surround myself
like Persephone
with flowers.

TABLEAUX OF THE JADE

1. A man is lowered into an excavated well
   to collect jade stones.
   Afterwards, he recovers from unconsciousness
   due to lack of oxygen.*

2. When the jade arises from the well,
   it is green, it is white,
   it is the leaves of winter cabbages.

3. A man is lowered into the jade.
   Observers on the black shore
   watch as he descends.

4. He descends. He descends.
   His pulse slows.
   His lungs freeze.

5. In the center of the jade there is a castle.
   In the castle sits a green prince,
   who greets the emissary calmly.

6. They drink tea in a white room.
   They exchange gifts.

7. When the man arises from the jade,
   he brings up oxygen,
   he brings up light.

8. He leaves his shadow in the jade.

9. Afterwards, he recovers from that loss.

*Caption of an illustration in the Avery Brundage collection,
San Francisco.

THE FIREFLIES

Midnight. The fireflies
tighten their circle around the house.
The children are leaping away
like moths in the moonlight
while side by side in their heavy bedroom
man and wife, wife and man
slumber like trees,
twin trees with black bark. . . .

One A.M. The fireflies approach.
Points of cold heat, exclamations of light,
they stitch the darkness like Morse code.
Now they play among leaves,
now they puncture thick bark.
Pine needles hiss in the forest:
already the robins have flown
and the children vanished in moonlight whiter than cream.

Flashing, the fireflies draw nearer.
It is almost their hour.

DAWN

A constellation of new lights.
The clock drops five clear notes
into the cold pool of the sky,
and the night peels away in layers—
old bark, old skin, old
heavy thought.

Birds rise,
flowers, trees, dew-colored boards, all
shimmering. And the sleepers
sink deeper into themselves:
darkness blooms on the inside of their skulls
like new fur.

IN THE FOURTH WORLD

in the fourth world
I grew wings and began to dance
in the fourth world
I started to write poems and couldn't stop
in the fourth world
my hair turned purple as the rings of Saturn
in the fourth world
I always knew who the murderer was
slept well woke early
didn't smoke
never ate too much
in the fourth world
my eyes were butterflies
opening
in the fourth world
someone I had never met before called me by my name
"come here a minute, Sandra"
and gave me a map on which was clearly marked
the way through suburbs airports deltas avenues
letters windmills tulips galaxies
to the fifth world
and the sixth world
and the seventh

IN THE FOURTH WORLD

was composed in Linotron 606 Baskerville by

Akra Data, Inc. of Birmingham, Alabama,

printed by McNaughton & Gunn, Inc. of Ann Arbor, Michigan,

and bound by John H. Dekker and Sons, Grand Rapids, Michigan.

Project Editor: Francis Squibb

Book design: Anna F. Jacobs with Dianne Pasquarelli

Production: Paul R. Kennedy